The Book of Ephesians

...a love story to the Gentiles

But now in Christ Jesus you (Gentiles) who once were far off
have been brought near by the blood of Christ.
Ephesians 2:13 (NKJV)

john eisner

Ruth's Road

www.ruthsroad.org

Scripture quotations are from the New King James Version of the Bible, unless otherwise specified. All emphasis are mine in quoted scripture. Copyright 1979, 1980, 1982, Thomas Nelson, Inc., Publisher.

Cover design: john eisner (with signature help from

Matt Worwood).

Ruth's Road logo design: Abigail Eisner

Finding the Afikoman

Preface

"I can't begin to explain the blindness that came off my eyes when I read my husband's book. For years I have heard John repeat the phrase, *"Jew and Gentile, one new man"* almost to the point of annoyance. His obsession with the book of Ephesians seemed "unbalanced" at times because I failed to understand John's unique assignment from the Lord. Now, as I read the fruit of his 40-year journey, I am undone by what has been hidden in secret and carried faithfully in John's heart to be given as a gift to the Body of Christ that John loves so much. I had no idea that I was in need of a deep healing from being born a Gentile. Because I was not Jewish, I was a disappointment to my in-laws. I was tolerated, even eventually loved, but always second choice. I was allowed, after deliberation, at family Seders because it was defiling to have a Gentile at your table. In the Jewish community I was "that Gentile girl" who influenced the Eisner's son to convert to Christianity. Messianic believers said I should change my Gentile name, Christie, meaning, "follower of Jesus" so I wouldn't be offensive to Jews. Even the scriptures confirmed that there was a huge advantage to being a Jew because they carried the riches of 4,000 years of culture and Biblical revelation that I have felt so blessed to be grafted into. They were the "first-born" and even in my own family line-up, I was second-born and I understood that means, "not quite as privileged" but that's ok. They were *God's chosen people* and I completely accepted the necessity, as well as the hardship, that comes with that calling. My mind, my words and the Bible affirmed that my identity was found in Jesus and that I was equal, but I had no idea how deep the inferiority and rejection from being a Gentile was until I read John's book. I still can't explain what happened to me... it was a deliverance and salvation rolled into one... and I can't stop crying. It was like John opened a door that I have never felt I had full access to, and with the love of the Father, he welcomed me in... as if to say, *'Where have you been? We have been waiting for you to take your honored seat at the table. We cannot begin until you take your place.'*

I believe that the Father has revealed to John His heart in "the mystery of one new man" and it will set you free."

Christie Eisner

dedication

As I contemplated writing a good and meaningful dedication, I could have made an impressive list of people I have read or barely known, which would in some way have given me more credibility. Then of course I could dedicate it to God, and that's always a sure fire winner. So instead I settled on the real dedication, and that's my wife Christie. What she has done in secret for most of our marriage, since we became believers, was to carry her heart daily before the Lord. That secret life of hers undergirded our family over the years and allowed me the luxury of developing my own heart in a home with a conducive atmosphere for the presence of the Lord. She also did more than just encourage me, but was able to put my life in context and help me see what I was blind to. The things that I at times saw as unrelated events, she was able to recognize God weaving a 'story' for His glory into it all. For years I carried a sense of Jew and Gentile and one new man, but never took it as being significant; I just saw it as things I 'rambled on' about. Finally Christie challenged me to begin writing my thoughts down in the form of a book. It all seemed like too much work and self-importance, so for quite a while I managed to ignore her prodding. She has been so to speak "the wind under my wings" (sorry for using that, but it worked here); she has always been supportive of my writing style, but she wanted Holy Spirit to have freedom to draw out what was uniquely in my heart. So thank you Christie, even if this work never ends up in anyone's hands, you made it possible; you showed your love for me in the process and your desire for Jesus to get His due reward, in all of its forms. God has surely given me one of His special treasures, when he brought you into my life. je

Introduction

What could I possibly have been thinking when I considered writing anything concerning the glorious Book of Ephesians, without at least a master's degree in theology? Do we really need another book among the thousands already written? Before I answer these questions, let me go back to my 'beginnings'. My parents escaped the atrocities of Hitler and the Nazis in around 1938. The only place at the time that would receive the 125,000 Jews fleeing extermination was Shanghai, China. My grandparents, aunts, uncles, and cousins, had tickets for passage six weeks later. Unfortunately their tickets would, at best, serve as kindling for the fires of Hitler's ovens, and set ablaze their innocent bodies as part of his plan to exterminate the Jewish 'vermin' of Europe. At that time Shanghai was not the modern, prosperous city of today. When my parents arrived it was considered a third world city, under Japanese occupation. Traumatized by the loss of homeland, family and friends, my parents, Hildegard and Bernard, were determined to survive, in spite of their difficult circumstances. After being released from the Japanese refugee camp, they found a one-room apartment in the general population among the local Chinese. To help ends meet, they rented out their space to some Russian, Jewish musicians, as a place to rehearse. Hildegard's 'kitchen' was a small hibachi grill outside on the street, where the sewage from the neighborhood freely ran by. Bernard meanwhile repaired bicycles and typewriters, until the American army liberators hired him to drive trucks full of TNT.

As if living with the daily torment of not knowing the fate of their family members left behind in Germany wasn't enough, they suffered the tragic loss of my three year old sister, Miriam. She died from amebic dysentery, due to the unsanitary conditions that surrounded their lives. Nine long years later, they immigrated to the US, leaving behind the grave of their precious Miriam; with their precocious four year old, Ellen, at their side, and a baby (me) in Hildegard Eisner's womb.

I grew up in a lower-class neighborhood in Denver, Colorado, speaking German before learning English. My life was surrounded by other Holocaust 'survivors' with heavy accents and Nazi number tattoos scribbled on their arms. I was always aware of being 'different'. Beside my perceived stigma of having immigrant parents, I had no relatives beyond my sister and parents...no grandparents; no aunts and uncles; no cousins; no family reunions. My parents were conservative Jews, mostly culturally oriented toward Judaism and its traditions. I went to Hebrew school as a young child and had a Bar Mitzvah at 13. In my teens and beyond I drifted away from my faith and heritage, and just wanted to be like everyone else around me. At times I was embarrassed by how different my mother and father were from the other 'regular' kids parents at school.

The 60's brought further opportunity to 'drift away' into a world of drugs and rock and roll (oh my what a cliché; wasn't I original!). When I married Christie in 1974, I finally had a soul-mate, to travel this road of life with. Of course we didn't know what the 'road' was, but we were happy. Christie, worked hard to be accepted by my parents and to understand them, though they seemed like they were from another planet, compared to the Gentile world she grew up in.

During this time of the early 70's, Christie and I became uncomfortable with all that was going on in our generation. In our own way we began to 'cry out' for help and as it says in Exodus 3: "God heard our cry, and came down to deliver us". The year was 1976 in a home church in Boulder Colorado, and that encounter with the Jewish Man, Christ Jesus, has kept us, until this very day; increasing in love for God and desiring His presence daily. Wow, what an awesome God we serve! We didn't realize it at the time, but the Lord saw me as a Jewish man, who believed in the Promised Messiah of the Jewish people. Even in that, though He was 'marking' my identity as a believer and as a Jew; I was pretty much oblivious. As a new Christian, I was so glad to finally 'belong' to something with real substance and life. I loved the church that Jesus made me a part of. There was no sense of me being a Jew or Jesus being one. Jesus was a "Christian", and I was following Him and I really liked His friends.

Over the years there were those, when they discovered my Jewish identity, that thought it was fitting for Christie and I to be in a Messianic congregation, but I felt no need to be. I loved the church as I had come to know it, and it was just such a gift for me to be a part of all these people without any 'unnecessary' Jewish trappings. After all, Jesus had set me free! Discovering my Jewish identity has been a 40 year journey. In short, I just want to emphasize that over the years I have had an ongoing love affair with Jesus and His church. I should add here that during this same time, Christie was looking for Jesus in the Jewish/biblical feasts and taking care of my mom and being exposed to the Jewish community in Denver. So as her heart grew in hunger and understanding of how the Lord viewed these things, I was more than oblivious, and just involved with growing as a believer in Jesus. Oh how the 'free will of man' is so swallowed up in the sovereignty of God! He must be continually smiling as He makes our lives something beautiful.

I would like to proceed on to the next 'beginning'; even though until recently I didn't know it was a beginning. In the early 80's I was a dental technician and Christie and I were in the process of moving to Loveland, Colorado, where I had gotten a new job at a small dental lab. At that time, I was also going through what you might call an introspective process with the Lord. I was in need of an encounter from the living God and revelation from above. I needed something more than merely repeating truths I had been told as a new believer in Jesus. I wanted to really know Him! One evening, I found myself alone in the lab. Everyone else had left for the day and I was sitting there alone with the lights out and the radio on. The station was tuned to NPR, _All Things Considered_, and they were discussing the death of a 'great' guru in India; who was being heralded as greater than Gandhi. He was known for representing all the great spiritual 'masters' in history, (which of course included Jesus, in this line-up) and the people adored and worshiped this man. He was especially known for asking his devotees from the upper castes to give up 10% of their land. In turn he would give it to the "landless poor" that lovingly followed him. At this point, I turned off the radio and in the silence, turned to the Lord. _"So Father, I know by everything I have been told, that I am saved and this guru wasn't... even though he claimed you as one of the 'ones' he believed in. Yet, the good works he did to bring redemption to others far exceed my own. Help me understand this; I really need to know!"_ I sat there in the silence and gradual darkness of the evening, as I prepared to go home. I was feeling no expectation of really getting an answer; but suddenly, I heard a voice speaking to me. I was startled and began looking all over the room for the source of the 'voice'. I even glanced over toward a large plant across the room, thinking someone must be hiding there. Please understand, this was not an impression or 'internal voice'; this was a loud, clear, **audible** voice that spoke the following words: _"You are greater than this man; he has reconciled man to dirt and sentenced them to_ *death; you have been called to reconcile man to God and brothers one to another."*

So, a few minutes later I was in my car for my drive home. "What?", you might say. "You just had an audible word from the Lord, and you packed up your stuff and got in the car and drove home for the evening?" Yes, that was the case. No obvious transformation or sudden sense of my ultimate purpose in God. It was just another drive home after work. Sorry I can't work it up, I wish I had been 'slammed' to the floor...shook, wept or whatever; resulting in total transformation. In fact, now some forty years later, I can't say definitively what that was truly all about. Christie has been such a help and blessing to me, and has encouraged me that my dramatic encounter with God was the beginning of the message that has been gestating inside of me for 40 years. She is convinced that this book is part of the overflow of that experience. Now, looking back, I can see that I have had an inherent love for the church/ecclesia; and a desire to see people reconciled to God... But, now more than that, I have had a passion to see Jew and Gentile expressed as one new man. Yet, it wasn't like I have consciously developed a ministry of reconciling Jew and Gentile over the years. It is just what began to 'ooze' out of me, whether I realized it or not.

For years at IHOPKC (International House of Prayer, Kansas City), I would push pass my aversion to speaking on a microphone and pray at intercession sets for Israel and 'one new man'. It's not like I had developed a clear theology about what the expression of the two joined as one was to look like, but I got up and prayed out of my heart and God's Word. I remember one

Sunday at a 6am set, getting up and praying that God would awaken the church in Yemen to cry out for the salvation of the small Jewish community in that war-torn nation. I felt it was like the hidden catalyst that would strengthen the struggling, persecuted church there; as Jew and Gentile stood together, before the powers and principalities that had taken them all hostage. The realization or revelation that the Jew, so to speak, was the missing ingredient in a 'cosmic chemistry experiment'; by adding the Jew to the believing Gentiles, the power and dynamics of the church would change! That is why God, I now believe, would not let me abandon the mostly Gentile, church body.

The Lord used Christie's journey of finding Jesus in the Leviticus 23 feasts, to help point the way back to my identity as a Biblical Jew, but it was my past 40+ years of walking with Jesus in a predominantly Gentile, Greek thinking church, that gave me the rich inheritance of knowing Jesus. Now, in deep gratitude to my Gentile brothers and sisters, who, for 2,000 years carried the revelation that Jesus is the Jewish Messiah that died for my sin: you carried this message of salvation through persecution, hardship, and often times so dark that only a flicker of this glorious flame of truth still remained; and yet you did your job faithfully; just as God planned from the foundation of the world, and you gave it to me. Now, it is my turn, as a Jewish believer to give back to you an inheritance that is rightfully yours and mine. A treasure that has been hidden by God's sovereign plan, for 2 millennia, but now it is time for you to receive this glorious gift.

So I offer this 'little book' from Ephesians to you; God's love story to the Gentiles. I have carried what I believe to be His heart and now I humbly pray that He will impart it to yours. I felt such tenderness towards my Gentile brothers and sisters as I wrote this…a real 'giddiness' at the prospect that what I was feeling was more than nice thoughts. So I offer to you what I believe is the genuine love of God speaking to your hearts. Oh dear Gentile believers, may you be encouraged and built up reading this offering. May you be lost in the wonder of God's incredible, limitless love for you. May we, together begin to experience what has been lost to His beautiful bride over the last two thousand years, and may we dare to believe that the Living God…the Holy One of Israel, has a magnificent plan! It is a plan that has been hidden for the ages, and will now be revealed to and **through** the ecclesia; which is Jesus' beautiful bride, Jew and Gentile, across the entire earth.

If you find yourself reading my book on the Book of Ephesians, I am truly humbled, that you would allow me to share the love of God, through my inadequate words.

Thank you, john e

Ephesians

The book of Ephesians; a new kind of love story...the Father sent His love to the Gentile nations so He could prepare a beautiful bride for His beloved son. Even as man and woman are joined in marriage to become one flesh; so too, are Jew and Gentile in Christ. Though distinct, they are equal; yet the 'union' holds a mystery to be revealed by the 'ecclesia' in the future.

*note: I don't mean to get into a controversy about the use of words; that can become a distraction. However, I feel it is important to address a misconception reflected in the use of the word, 'church'. This word does not actually exist in the bible. It is merely a construct that was added many years after the New Testament was written and recorded. Instead, I will be using the word, 'ecclesia'; which is the Greek word used in the original. I am not doing this to create an issue, but rather to make a distinction in terms and intent. The word 'ecclesia' is not a New Testament term. The basic meaning of this Greek word is: a meeting place or gathering where the citizens could speak their minds and try to influence one another. In religious groups you could say it could make a distinction between an institutional gathering and intentional heart gatherings. Even before the time of Jesus, Jews who wanted to explore what they felt were deeper issues in their faith would gather as ecclesia, as opposed to the more formalized synagogue. One example of this type of gathering among the Jews, could be Essenes. This is in no way to say they were more 'right' or holy, but they expressed a heart response that caused them to, let's say gather, or *ecclesia*. So, for the sake of allowing me to express my thoughts, indulge me while you are reading this and use 'ecclesia' anywhere you see the word, 'church'. Again, not to impugn two thousand years of church history, but maybe to focus on the motive and intent of those doing the gathering. So for now, every time you see the word 'church' in your translation, substitute the word 'ecclesia'... say it 10 times and don't worry about how you pronounce it, just get used to the word. Ecclesia; ecclesia; ecclesia; ecclesia; ecclesia; ecclesia; ecclesia; ecclesia; ecclesia; ecclesia. Now that wasn't so hard, and you didn't lose your salvation.

Now as we proceed, please close your commentaries and other writings about the book of Ephesians. Open your heart as we go on this journey into what the Father, for so long, has kept hidden in His heart; yes, what He wanted all along.

So Saul, as a young man found himself at the forefront (at least he thought so) of God's stand against this heresy of a Jewish Man, Jesus; claiming to be, of all things, the Jewish Messiah! I wonder how many of the respected elders and shepherds of Israel at the time, laid their robes at the feet of this zealous young man (Acts 7:58). Did Stephen make 'knowing' eye contact with Saul as the rocks hit their mark, in his execution as a heretic? Oh, how emboldened young Saul's heart must have been; what 'heady' company he must have been keeping. *"If only I was of age, I too could have hurled a stone, instead of just being a witness...!"* The die was cast; he knew what great calling lay ahead. It would take years of further education and devotion to be properly 'armed' with God's word and the understanding received from the great rabbis of His people. He wanted confidence in doing the will of the Holy One of Israel. He wanted to put away this scourge that was affecting his holy community. These followers of this false messiah must be dealt with; either with words from the Holy Scriptures...or with stones coming from righteous men's hands. They are a blight in our community... what a high calling; what a privilege to serve the Living God in this way! They must be stopped; they must be eradicated! God's beloved first-born son (Israel) is being attacked and deceived; but God in His mercy has sent a 'deliverer': young Saul of Tarsus!

As Saul's renown and authority increased, in 'breathing' threats and murder against these disciples of the false Jewish Messiah, he got permission to go to Damascus. This 'cancer' had spread beyond the gates of Jerusalem; he must go and save his people! There were great sacrifices and hardships Saul had to endure to complete the two hundred and twenty-five mile trek to Damascus (Acts 9). Intense desert heat and terrain, and then there were the bandits and robbers... *"But I count it all gain, to serve the Living God of Israel, for His name's sake; for His beloved holy people Israel"*. What's this! What's this bright light? "Saul, Saul, why are you persecuting Me"? "Who are You Lord"? Then, the incredible inconvenient answer came: "I am Jesus, Whom you are persecuting"! As we approach the book of Ephesians, can we be prepared for such an 'inconvenient' encounter, also? Can we allow some of our preconceived ideas be challenged by God's word? Saul knew how to respond to the Mighty God of Israel, his life and community prepared him for this moment. Trembling and astonished, he said, "Lord, what do you want me to do"? (Oh, to have a willing, obedient heart that recognizes the presence of the Lord enough to respond like that; not to be bound by my personal zeal or theology. Lord, give me that kind of heart.) "Arise and go"! What more could Saul or us ever need?

Acts 9:8 (NKJV) *8 Then Saul arose from the ground, and when his eyes were opened he saw no one. But they led him by the hand and brought him into Damascus.*

Then Saul arose from the ground (he was overcome by the Spirit of God), and when he opened his eyes, he realized he couldn't see. So now begins his 'school of the Spirit' and discipleship to represent God to his people (at least that's probably what he thought at this point; being sent to the Gentiles, would have been totally out of his comprehension).

Acts 9:9 (NKJV) *⁹ And he was three days without sight, and neither ate nor drank.*

So he was blind for three days (he didn't read any commentaries to explain what was happening to him, or theology of Who Jesus was) and fasted food and water. Then the Lord sends a servant; a believer in Jesus, Ananias (Hananiah) to pray for Saul. (Keep in mind, that Ananias has more information about Saul's/Paul's calling then he does himself.)

Acts 9:15 (NKJV) *¹⁵ But the Lord said to him, "Go, for he is a chosen vessel of Mine to bear My name before Gentiles, kings, and the children of Israel.*

God also mercifully prepares Saul for what is about to take place, by giving him a vision of Ananias. He gives him a vision; but not vision…! Ananias arrives, prepared by the Lord to know what to do and who this guy is to become, yet standing before him is a powerful man with authority given to him by the chief priest to arrest Jews like himself. (Also, keep in mind at this point of biblical history, neither Saul/Paul, nor Ananias were considering that Gentiles would believe in the Jewish

Messiah Jesus. Gentiles were so involved in darkness and unclean lifestyles, they couldn't even eat with them; let alone be in community with them.) What was Ananias' heart doing with the words Holy Spirit had spoken to him concerning Saul…? "To bear My name before Gentiles…"? Wow! Ananias goes to the house Paul is staying at; lays hands on him and…?

Acts 9:17 (NKJV) *17 And Ananias went his way and entered the house; and laying his hands on him he said, "Brother Saul, the Lord Jesus, who appeared to you on the road as you came, has sent me that you may receive your sight and be filled with the Holy Spirit."*

No preparation; no teaching; just God-given authority! The scales were gone and he received his sight and straight away as a 'good Jew' he went to a mikvah (Jewish, ritual immersion facility) and got baptized; completely immersed, ritually and spiritually cleansed! So there you have Paul's training program: he immediately went to the synagogue and preached Christ; that He, Jesus is the promised Messiah; the Son of the Holy One of Israel…yet, still no Gentiles in his sights. He had a very specific 'audience':

Acts 9:22 (NKJV) *22 But Saul increased all the more in strength, and confounded the **Jews** who dwelt in Damascus, proving that this Jesus is the Christ.*

Now the leadership of the Jewish community in Damascus in response to Paul's new mission to the Jews began plotting to kill him. It must have been so surreal for him, whom, as a young man was party to the death of Stephen for the same 'offense' he was now being accused of. Having been made aware of their plans, he escaped and went to Jerusalem. Of course he was met with a little suspicion and fear among the brethren in Jerusalem; after functioning with some of them there, he was able to prove himself. The result of course was that the Hellenist Jews there wanted to kill him. Then, followed a special time for the believing community in Jesus of peace and edification (keep in mind again at this time…all Jews). They walked in the joy of the fear of the Lord; the comfort of the Holy Spirit; and they were multiplied (God's way).

About here you would expect Paul to have his big breakthrough with his heart and calling for the Gentiles…but first, God's chosen vessel to the Gentiles, Peter, takes over! I won't go into Peter's process here, but God prepared him for this endeavor with a dream (Acts 10). He would have definitely been in need of some 'divine' encouragement and intervention to be willing to say "yes" to this assignment to the Gentiles. It would have been unthinkable; the Gentiles were residents of darkness; how could they be candidates for being welcomed into the community of Jewish believers in Messiah Jesus; just beyond the pale. What in fact would they do with these converts, if indeed God had this in mind? *"We can't even have them in our homes for a meal; how could we possibly disciple them?* Holy Spirit 'shows up' to make sure there is no doubt that God is involved in this event (Acts 10: 44-47); this unheard of event! Because He confirmed it, they then could be baptized; just like the Jewish believers before them; in the mikvah (Hebrew word for ritual immersion; or as we would today say: 'baptism'). Even as late as Acts 13, Paul was still focusing on his Jewish brethren, teaching in synagogues…resulting in more Jewish believers in Israel.

Here now is Paul's turning point toward the Gentiles…

Acts 13:46 (NKJV) *⁴⁶ Then Paul and Barnabas grew bold and said, "It was necessary that the word of God should be spoken to you (Jews) first; but since you reject it, and judge yourselves unworthy of everlasting life, behold, we turn to the Gentiles*

So, we have finally 'made it'; Paul's Gentile journey begins. Let's now jump ahead to the book of Ephesians, to catch a glimpse of how God manifests this calling to the Gentiles through this unexpected willing vessel for the Lord of Glory.

I would encourage you to spend some time reading the first three chapters of Ephesians on your own; don't study it or refer to commentaries. Just read it devotionally and in one sitting as often as possible to get the narrative, take the whole thing in; explore God's heart for these people. Occasionally answer the question, "Who is he speaking to?" "Who is the 'you'?" "Who is the 'us'?" Who are the saints?" Let the context answer these questions; not your previous assumptions. It might even change at times depending on the context. This is a book expressing God's love and desire to and for the Gentiles and at the same time, on and off addressing the Jewish believers. God's heart for 'one new man' is reflected throughout; Jew and Gentile.

Note: I believe Paul wrote this book in layers and you will see and feel them as you read with an open heart. I will put labels in where I believe appropriate to give my sense of who the focus of the sentence or word is. This of course is speculative on my part (yet no more than the assumptions commentaries make in ignoring or minimizing the 'audience'), but I believe will help you slow down and consider the nuance of some of Paul's words. I may also present two 'variations' of who might be the subject of a section or verse. Please, again try not to get too theological as we read these verses, but get a feel of the implications and context, by allowing yourself to explore options in the context of these verses; let the 'narrative' of God's heart come out. There is so much to gain for our hearts and minds; allow for open conversations and explore the depth of God's heart.

- Jew and Gentile
- Jew
- Gentile

As I mentioned earlier I will be substituting the word 'ecclesia' for the word 'church', which is not meant to demean the church in anyway, just to help our minds again 'slow down' as we read and consider what is being said.

Ephesians 1:1 (NKJV) [1] Paul, an apostle of Jesus Christ by the will of God, To the saints (Jew and Gentile) who are in Ephesus, and faithful in Christ Jesus

Paul is writing from a place of God given authority. He is not just laying out theology; this is a journey of the heart. Push back on any clinical analysis; let Him speak to you from this 'place' that the Lord God Almighty, Himself has called Paul to. These are not just a smart man's opinions!

"To the saints" (Jew and Gentile)… if you keep in mind he is referring here to both the Jews and Gentiles in Ephesus, and if you were a Gentile believer in that city and had this mighty Jewish man of God include you as a 'saint' with his Jewish brethren, you would be very encouraged and thrilled. There had been a Jewish

presence in Ephesus for at least five generations (they were there before Jesus appearance as the "Suffering Servant" in the Gospels). The first believers in this city were only Jews...let that sink into your preconceived notions. This greeting is really a type of affirmation, ultimately to the Gentiles in that gathering. Paul is emphasizing their inclusion and standing with the Jewish believers in that city. The Jews originally were the only people in Ephesus that were associated with the Jewish Messiah, Jesus! Paul is now, referring to gentiles as 'saints' with the Jewish believing community He also called them "faithful in Christ Jesus"... a spiritual recognition that previously had been unheard of.

Before we leave these words that have become all too familiar to us: 'saints', 'faithful'...These Gentiles for the most part have just left a world of such utter darkness that we today would barely have a grid for. The types of behavior or forms of worship would today be considered so aberrant or perverted; we wouldn't even mention them in polite company. Yet in the setting of Greek gods and goddesses; it was 'normal' and you might even say sophisticated. These new Gentile believers had an encounter with the living God that was enough to deliver them from such darkness and the blood of Jesus cleansed their innermost being. But what about the practical implications of this experience? It may have been inwardly transformational, but how do these Gentiles relate to the original believers that were all Jews, especially at first? On the other hand, how could a Jewish family allow them to sit at their 'table' that was considered sacred? These people ate things sacrificed to demons; they did the unspeakable with temple prostitutes in what were considered forms of worship; men with men; men with animals, etc.! Have you ever wondered why in Acts 15, it says:

Acts 15 ²⁰ "...we write to them to abstain from things polluted by idols, *from* sexual immorality, *from* things strangled, and *from* blood.

That was their lifestyle and culture!. This wasn't meant to sum up all they ever had to consider giving up in this new 'walk' with the Jewish Messiah Jesus; it was just the first step in becoming part of this wondrously, glorious household of God, that they now found entrance into. How could they be 'discipled' and cared for if they couldn't enter each other's homes or be with their families and worship together; to celebrate the Lord of Glory? This wasn't about being in bondage; it was about removing barriers to fellowship. (Remember no commentaries, allow your heart and mind to consider what the scriptures actually are saying). Try to put yourself 'in the room'; what did the Gentiles feel; what did the Jewish believers feel? Have you ever taken the time to notice the next line says:

Acts 15 ²¹"*For Moses has had throughout many generations those who preach him in every city, being read in the synagogues every Sabbath.*"

What a strange verse! What could it be there for? Is it recognition of communities throughout the land of Israel with believing Jews that could be available for fellowship with these new Gentile converts…just wondering.

Ephesians 1:2 (NKJV) *2 to you (Jew and Gentile) and peace from God our Father and the Lord Jesus Christ*

The Lord God Almighty, the Holy One of Israel, is not mad at you, He is in your midst! Again, not to belabor the point; this is a 'gathering'; ecclesia that has never been witnessed in the history of the world! God's first born, that have been a living expression of His will and holiness upon the earth; standing now before all the world to see; Jew and Gentile. That the nations (Gentiles) have been brought into this 'household of the God of Israel'!

Note: how it began

Acts 10:15 (NKJV) *15 And a voice spoke to him again the second time, "What God has cleansed you must not call common."*

Peter's dream had nothing to do with food! This was a revelatory 'breaking in' of the Living God! He is declaring that through the blood of the Passover Lamb of God, a people who were considered so unclean that having a meal together was not allowed; even the mention of the kind of behavior that defined their lifestyle, was not permitted. Just speaking those things defiled the person making note of them or the 'hearers' of such words.

These unclean vessels are about to be included among this 'holy nation'! This ecclesia (not an institutional gathering), Jew and Gentile, is being addressed by one of the most respected and revered leaders of this believing community. Paul is letting it be known by both of them, Jew and Gentile:

Ephesians 2:2 *"Grace to you (Jew and Gentile) and peace from God our Father and the Lord Jesus Christ".*

To the Jew it was like the message that was delivered to Peter in Acts 10, and to the Gentile it was the most wonderful news; yet hard to imagine, with all the practical implications of this 'word'. The 'invitation' of God has now been publicly declared!

I need to add something here I wasn't planning on; I want to believe the Lord 'added' it to my heart this evening. I was watching the live stream of a small church (actually maybe an ecclesia) in Georgia, that seems to be having a visitation of Holy Spirit in their baptismal waters...fire of the Spirit in those waters! It's simple; a few people standing in the waters; a line of people lined up to enter the waters; worship playing in the background, and people in the congregation sitting and standing around praying or whatever. No teaching; preaching, yelling or anything of the sort. No grand entrance of the pastor, just a guy who must be somewhat in charge with a microphone, interviewing the people before they collapse or just give themselves to the 'waters'. This is what struck me; it was 'presence of God centered and people oriented'. Really not that much to see; no great emotion; just what appeared to be, a genuine concern for each individual who took the time to come there; whether from far or near. There are different races of men, women and children; small; large; rich and poor; old and young...just 'folks'. That was it... and I began to weep! What more could we want! So here we are looking at the book of Ephesians; one of the 'crown jewels' of the scriptures. Hundreds, maybe thousands of books written about it; untold sermons preached and analysis and conversation beyond number, but what is really happening here? A people gathered together in the presence of God, being told who they are and 'dunked' into the love of God; Jew and Gentile together, as never before! This is really such a simple book, if seen through the lens of God's love and not clouded by intellect and theology. An event recorded for all to see and desire; to hear the words...to experience the emotions; one year later; one hundred years later; two thousand years later. An event to take into our hearts and know what we are a part of; Jew and Gentile; one new man. Not just words to be dissected and analyzed for the purpose of satisfying our intellects. This is an identity that can be lived out; not merely a theology that can be argued.

Ephesians 1:3 (NKJV) *³ Blessed be the God and Father of our Lord Jesus Christ*

As these brethren (Jew and Gentile) stand before the Holy One of Israel, and are still trying to 'recover' from Paul's initial words; he re-focuses them on the One, that 'brought' them here; Who just gave them words of life! Yes, these are not just a mere man's words: "Blessed be the God and Father of our Lord Jesus Christ." This is not a church gathering; this is God's gathering His flock to declare His love and intentions over them; this is ecclesia. This is not one of the innumerable gods, that the Gentiles in this gathering, used to worship. Take a moment: "Blessed be the God and Father of our Lord Jesus Christ, Who has brought us into this same 'place'; we step into this moment in the spirit with these Jewish and Gentile brethren. Thank you! Thank you!"

Ephesians 1:3 (NKJV) *who has blessed us with every spiritual blessing in the heavenly places in Christ*

Again, Paul is emphasizing this union of the Spirit; Gentiles included with the believing Jews of Ephesus. Not partial promises; not just the Jews; not just the Gentiles; every blessing in heavenly places... in the true sanctuary of God in heavenly places... Gentiles fully included; open wide the heavenly gates! Not 'second class' citizens! This was so unheard until the Lord of Glory sent out men like Peter and Paul from the believing Jewish community. We could camp out here and unpack all the implications of this and possibly never leave, but again consider the 'audience' here and the affect upon the hearts and minds of both the Jews and Gentiles. They were given all the blessings! Many of the Jewish believers couldn't imagine sharing this standing, before the Lord God, King of Kings, with these defiled people. The Gentiles that have now found their way into this holy abode through the blood of Jesus, are expecting to be considered second-class citizens at best. Every blessing in heavenly places! Every blessing in heavenly places! Can you even imagine what this must have been like for these new Gentile believers in Ephesus? They didn't just 'crawl across the threshold' into family of God; they were lifted up, carried in upon the shoulders of Paul and the others and given a full place at the 'table'. They were 'carried' in by the word of God and thousands of years of the Jewish people 'carrying' that word! As we shall see later, it was as necessary for them to be here as it was for the Jewish brethren to accept them; no, not just accept, but fully embrace them as equal, yet distinct members of one another! The Father shall have a beautiful and perfect bride for His Beloved Son; Jew and Gentile!

Note: in verse 1:4, I can see the "us" being Jew or Jew and Gentile, so here is the first reading with Jew:

Ephesians 1:4 (NKJV) *4 just as He chose us (Jew and Gentile) in Him before the foundation of the world, that we (Jew and Gentile) should be holy and without blame before Him in love.*

So again to begin with, just remember Paul is addressing the congregation made up of both Jew and Gentile; each one will be seeing and feeling these words from their own perspective. To these Gentiles, it again is Paul 'blowing their minds' and including them, not just in the present; rather in God's original intent. God's love for them, spanned over the centuries, even while they were in utter darkness and now being manifested for all to see. Paul is further reinforcing their value and unseen history, as they stand here with their Jewish brethren in Ephesus. Remember, no competition here; just God's pleasure for those standing before, this never before 'ecclesia': Jew <u>and</u> Gentile! The result of this new declaration over their lives, is not just to produce some kind of theoretical or theological standing, but *"holy and without blame before Him in love"*. Did he say holy and without blame? For the Jews to hear this, could produce such a 'shaking' at their very foundations; this was their promise and inheritance! How could these ones rescued from the clutches of the darkest of live styles, be given this standing with "God's first born"? For the Gentile members of this gathering; the recognition that they weren't just second class 'citizens', but fully receiving God's grace and standing before him... and, of course the result is "love"! This is not just a quiz or legal truth; this love is real and enduring; Paul's words have the authority of God upon them, to produce a people: Jew and Gentile that He has been waiting for since before the foundation of the world.

And now for the "Jew" version of this verse (meaning that the "us" is read as meaning "Jews"):

Ephesians 1:4 (NKJV) *4 "Just as He chose us (Jews) in Him before the foundation of the world, that we (Jews) should be holy and without blame before Him in love."*

This may take a few 'readings' of the verse. Slow down and read it, spend time with it and picture Paul speaking to the Jews, specifically in the room. By addressing the Jews alone here, he is 'setting up' the next verses and adding weight to them. He could be saying the "us" here emphasizing his relationship to the Jews, so he can move with added authority to what was to follow. The "us" gets strengthened so that the "we" (Jew and Gentile), will really drive home the reality of what the Gentiles have been brought into. Allow yourself to become aware of this 'back and forth' that Paul does, with the three options we discussed earlier. Don't just gloss over the implications of this; remember the Gentiles were brought into something holy and special. It wasn't like they just wandered into a church and got 'saved'. They were excluded for thousands of years; he isn't putting the Gentiles down, but actually elevating them. You (Gentiles) are now invited into what was originally thought of as just for "us" (Jews), from before the foundation of the earth. This is a big deal; a really big deal! Come on now, "holy and without blame before Him in love"...! A Gentile included in this...are you kidding me? Maybe allow them to be servants cleaning up after us... but "holy and blameless"? Wow! Let's now move on to the next verses.

Ephesians 1:5 (NKJV) *⁵ having predestined us (Jew and Gentile);*

Moving on to the 'inclusive' "us", Paul is looking across the room; overwhelmed with love for these Gentile believers, now included with the Jews in Ephesus. Yes the Lord God Almighty, Himself has determined this day, this expression, when He planned the entire creation. Wake up you angels, and behold this beautiful bride; Jew and Gentile, being prepared for the King of glory; the Lord Jesus Christ Himself! Dear Gentile brethren, you were "predestined" to be included in this company of God's chosen ones; one new man. The "us" here is an expression of humility and authority on Paul's part. If you are a Gentile and are reading this, let the depth of the standing before your heavenly Father, penetrate your heart! A standing that is not merely theological, or solely based two thousand years of 'church' history; but from before the foundation of the earth! If you don't 'see' the Jewish believer in the 'room'; you won't feel the weight of what you are a part of. Soak it in!

Ephesians 1:5 *"…to adoption as sons by Jesus Christ to Himself"*

First of all, biblical adoption is a total change of name and identity. You become fully a part of the new 'family', with no association with the old man. As a son; "by Jesus Christ to Himself!" Not as a servant, but as an equal to His chosen ones…not by the will of man; not by works; not merely political or social standing; not by your own strength. No, but by the will of God and for God; so we can rejoice in His glorious ways. It's by His grace; by Jesus Himself, His blood and the power of the Holy Spirit. Accepted; accepted; Jew and Gentile; in the Beloved! Not a denomination or church gathering; but into Him; unto Him! (note: the Jew may be the first-born, and though now you are also considered a 'son'; you don't supplant the Jew, but have an equal, yet unique position as a Gentile.)

Ephesians 1:5 (NKJV)…*according to the good pleasure of His will*

Hear His heart; don't go into theological analysis; it's His Heart! It's the pleasure of God to do this; spend some time here; 'dive in'. You Gentiles are here in this glorious body because He gets pleasure in you be included with His Jewish brethren. He's not just checking the appropriate boxes and Paul isn't dryly making up a bunch of rules. This is a love story of epic proportions!

More love and blessing coming your way, oh you Gentiles and Jews who have been knit together in the tender heart of the Maker of heaven and earth...

Ephesians 1:6 (NKJV) *6 to the praise of the glory of His grace, by which He has made us accepted in the Beloved.*

(Resist the temptation to 'jump' into that theology pool that continually beckons you)...Paul is just helping you receive the embrace of God and accept the truths he just told you about. It is His grace; His kindness by which He has made you more than merely "accepted" in a legal sense; you, Jew and Gentile friends, have been endowed with the grace of God! You are the recipient of the graciousness of the Living God...that is being worked out in your weak flesh and blood. Not by your great efforts, but rather the supernatural grace of God, being worked out in your life, by His life working in you. Put away the 'quiz' you keep trying to get right to be "accepted in the Beloved", and let Holy Spirit have His way in you; for His pleasure. Here they are again, standing shoulder-to-shoulder, Jew and Gentile; receiving the love of God spoken over them by this servant of the Living God, Paul.

Ephesians 1:7 (NKJV) *⁷ In Him we (Jew and Gentile) have redemption through His blood, the forgiveness of sins, according to the riches of His grace…the redemption speaks of a debt paid by the blood of Jesus.*

So here they are, these Jews and Gentiles, being 'washed' by the words spoken by Paul. Their hearts had to be starting to be 'melted' together; drenched in His love and experiencing His grace manifested in this love. Not just legally tolerating each other…could love for one another begin to melt the ice; the realization that the 'dividing wall' has been removed? The sins that made the Jews look like hypocrites to the unwashed Gentiles, and the sins that made the Gentiles so unacceptable to the Jewish members of the household of God. What legal agreements and edicts could not accomplish, the blood; the precious blood of the Lamb of God, has once and for all done. Here they are, standing together; Jew and Gentile, 'drenched' in this blood and falling in love, even as they are loved. "In Him we" (Jew & Gentile)… Let the 'Jew in' and allow yourself, if you are a Gentile, to see them standing beside you here… making the Lord's heart rejoice, seeing what He waited for: you Gentile brethren to be included with His brethren! If the Jew wasn't here, neither would you (Gentiles) be; think on that and get ready for the next verse.

Ephesians 1:9 (NKJV) *⁹ having made known to us the mystery of His will, according to His good pleasure which He purposed in Himself*

Oh how we are so capable of conditioned to just keep reading and not stop to take in this 'glory hole' of God's love! What is this 'mystery' that has brought the Lord of glory pleasure and He has committed Himself (Father, Son and Holy Spirit) to accomplish it! You are standing here in Ephesus, Jew and Gentile, and Paul now mentions the 'mystery'…what could it be? Look around; you are it: Jew and Gentile together. Not an institution or theology; but a living reality, the 'pleasure of God' expressed in flesh and blood before all the nations so they can bow before the Creator of heaven and earth. I can't do justice to this 'mystery' but I hope to stir you to consider going there with Holy Spirit and exploring it and allowing your heart to begin to take in what you are a part of (Jew and Gentile).

In the following we may have to slow our thinking down a bit and let the scriptures 'speak' rather that our preconceived notions of what is said here.

Ephesians 1:10 (NKJV) *10 that in the dispensation of the fullness of the times He might gather together in one all things in Christ, both which are in heaven and which are on earth--in Him.*

My goal is not to explore the depths of every verse, but

just take your heart on a bit of a journey. Books could be written on this verse and most in this wonderful book…"*He might gather together in one all things in Christ*": I want to submit to you here, that this 'one' is Jew and Gentile, One New Man. It's not about theology or denominations; it's a living reality when His bride (Jew and Gentile) stand before him; it's 'ecclesia' not church; it can not contained in buildings and mere declarations. Can you even begin to imagine what must be on God's heart for us to bring "both which are in heaven and which are on earth--in Him"…this is who we are! We aren't just waiting around for heaven; both the things in heaven and earth are established in us through Christ! You want a 'mystery' to contemplate for the rest of your life…well that should keep you pretty busy for a while! (I don't want to be dogmatic or impose a formula, but this 'mystery' is tied up in Jew and Gentile, which we have yet to see in our times.)

You might want to take a break here and worship Him for about a week…

Ephesians 1:11 (NKJV) *[11] In Him also we (Jew and Gentile) have obtained an inheritance, being predestined according to the purpose of Him who works all things according to the counsel of His will.*

I won't spend much time here but again think about what this must have sounded like to these new Gentile converts; "*obtained an inheritance*"…an inheritance going back thousands of years that is rooted in the

Jewish believers standing next to them. These Gentiles were uniquely prepared to worship with their entire beings as these truths came upon them by the words of Paul and the power of Holy Spirit. In the same sentence these Gentiles got another little emotional 'upgrade': "predestined". **Historically they have come in a bit late, but their 'place' was reserved in advance,** *"according to the purpose of Him who works all things according to the counsel of His will"!* Gentile reader, take a moment and put yourself in the 'room' with these brethren and let it wash over you; take your place next to these Jewish believers and receive the love and desire of the Living God for you as a Gentile; not to dominate the Jew or in a paternalist fashion pray for their salvation…but 'stand' next to them and enjoy the place God has made for you, from before the foundation of the earth. You have a 'predestined' inheritance that is yours (Gentile) to discover and live out of in your relationship with Father, Son and Holy Spirit.

Get ready, take a breath and let this verse speak for itself:

Ephesians 1:12 (NKJV) *12 that we (Jews) who first trusted in Christ should be to the praise of His glory.*

Yes Jews! Who in the 'room' first trusted? Who in Ephesus "first trusted"? Remember the congregation in

Ephesus is not just Gentiles...so again; who first trusted. Don't reach for the commentary! What does it say; not what you inductively say it says. Us Jews first believed so you Gentiles have something to become a part of. Where did your inheritance in the previous verse come from? Now get this: the Jews get "to be to the praise of His glory" because the Gentiles have "obtained an inheritance" so they could share this space; side by side in Ephesus. We (Jew and Gentile) have obtained!

(I want to add something I was feeling recently as I read through Ephesians: beginning in verse 3, I 'see' Paul standing before his gathering, and reaching out his arms, and embracing the whole room of Gentiles. His heart is overflowing with love, full of the promise and potential he feels for them, and he is reciting from a heavenly view, who they are meant to be. Then in verse 12, in complete humility, he says:

"12 that we (Jews) who first trusted in Christ should be to the praise of His glory"

that without you Gentiles, we Jews could not come to that place, reserved from before the beginning of time, that a people (Jew and Gentile), would gather together on the earth, "to the praise of His glory"! The Jew needs the Gentile; the Gentile needs the Jew; for God's sake.)

Ephesians 1:13 (NKJV) 13 In Him you (Gentiles) also trusted, after you (Gentiles) heard the word of truth, the gospel of your (Gentiles) salvation; in whom also having *believed, you (Gentiles) were sealed with the Holy Spirit of promise*

The last verse 'sets up' this verse. Go back and read it again; slowly, read what is written and not how you may have been told to consider this verse.   This is not a book of theology, though it has been turned into one by many. **This is a love story to Gentiles to help them become part of the biblical community that loves Jesus the Jewish Messiah.** Paul is helping them believe that the Lord God Almighty, the King of Kings loves them and has made a special place in His heart and His purposes upon the earth.

You (Gentiles) were *"sealed with the Holy Spirit of promise"*...if you are hearing this as a newly grafted in Gentile you are struggling to receive such an incredible gift that you thought was reserved only for God's chosen people (Jews)... something that you could observe from afar; but Paul is saying now that the blood of Jesus has not only delivered me (Gentile) from my utter dark existence. But He has also given me (Gentile) the very Holy Spirit that before now, we had only heard about. As a Jew in the room, I may be struggling. On the one hand, I know the power and love of God to transform; but these Gentiles; how could it be that the One that is so pure and holy, be 'given' to them? Yet, their apostolic leaders in the Jerusalem council came to the conclusion, that indeed, the Gentiles were 'fellow heirs' because of the Holy Spirit:

Acts 15:8-9 (NKJV) *⁸ So God, who knows the heart, acknowledged them by **giving them the Holy Spirit**, just as He did to us, ⁹ and made **no distinction** between us and them, purifying their hearts by faith…*(keep in mind this isn't the 15ᵗʰ chapter of the Book of Acts to these Jewish believers; this is recent history and official words from their leaders…!

Ephesians 1:14 (NKJV) *¹⁴ "Who is the guarantee of our (Jew)(Jew and Gentile) inheritance until the redemption of the purchased possession, to the praise of His glory.*

Again, Paul is encouraging and including the Gentiles in the 'our'…(not just theology). Don't forget what this must sound like to the Gentiles, who have only seen at best from afar this 'inheritance in the saints'; but now they are partakers of this inheritance, recipients; fully grafted into the household of God. They weren't just repeating a truth, but experiencing this 'guarantee' in the Holy Spirit, Who isn't a theology, but a living reality that has an affect on those He touches. An 'alternate' reading could put the our as the Jews, again including the Gentiles in what before was specifically thought of as being for the Jews alone, but also tying the Gentiles to a sense of 'inheritance'; being grafted in.

What follows; Ephesians 1: 15-23 would takes volumes to 'unpack' and my goal here is not to even begin to understand or explain it; I am just dealing with this is of "who is Paul speaking to". These verses are prayed and taught all over the world, but do we ever stop and ask who the 'your' and 'you' is that Paul is referring to? Let's 'dive in'!

Ephesians 1:15-23 (NKJV) *¹⁵ Therefore (because of the preceding) I also, after I heard of your (Gentiles) faith in the Lord Jesus and your (Gentiles) love for all the saints (Jews), ¹⁶ do not cease to give thanks for you (Gentiles), making mention of you (Gentiles) in my prayers: ¹⁷ that the God of our Lord Jesus Christ, the Father of glory, may give to you (Gentiles) the spirit of wisdom and revelation in the knowledge of Him, ¹⁸ the eyes of your (Gentiles) understanding being enlightened; that you (Gentiles) may know what is the hope of His calling, what are the riches of the glory of His inheritance in the saints (Jews), ¹⁹ and what is the exceeding greatness of His power toward us (Jews and Gentiles) who believe, according to the working of His mighty power ²⁰ which He worked in Christ when He raised Him from the dead and seated Him at His right hand in the heavenly places, ²¹ far above all principality and power and might and dominion, and every name that is named, not only in this age but also in that which is to come. ²² And He put all things under His feet, and gave Him to be head over all things to the ecclesia, ²³ which is His body, the fullness of Him who fills all in all.*

Once again Paul is not just doing theology; he is encouraging and caring for the Gentiles that he has been given the grace and authority to bring them into the biblical community in Ephesus! (Sometime we may also address the issue of there being no church at this point; just ecclesia; which is a response of the heart and not an institution…) There is an 'ocean' in these verses that I am not going to address, but even if you can read these verses in a new and maybe unfamiliar way, according to the actual context; then we have made progress that would be phenomenal, considering that the traditional reading of them would have a completely different understanding. Can you allow yourself for Holy Spirit speaking to you about these verses instead of Orthodox Christianity? Paul's desire is to totally 'blow their minds' about what they have now become a part of; it not only addresses present issues in their relationship to the community they have been grafted into; but all eternity! Let's take a breath and move on.

Ephesians 2:1-2 (NKJV) *¹ And you (Gentiles) He made alive, who were dead in trespasses and sins, ² in which you (Gentiles) once walked according to the course of this world, according to the prince of the power of the air, the spirit who now works in the sons of disobedience*

Paul, is turning to the Gentiles in the room; to encourage them, and make it clear to the Jewish brethren, that these, formerly unclean Gentiles, are now included in the 'household of God'. According to the course of this world, according to the prince of the power of the air…more lifting up of the Gentiles here; this dark lifestyle you (Gentiles) have been taken out of, isn't just because you (Gentiles) are so horrible, but it's the 'course of the world' and a powerful spirit is 'breathing' on this horrible life they (Gentiles) have been taken out of!

Ephesians 2:3 (NKJV) *³ among whom also we (Jews) all once conducted ourselves (Jews) in the lusts of our (Jews) flesh, fulfilling the desires of the flesh and of the mind, and were by nature children (Jews) of wrath, just as the others (Gentiles)*

Paul is indirectly answering the heart issues of the Jews in the room: "We (Jews) too are sinners in need of Jesus; just like the Gentiles in the 'room'", our new brothers and sisters in the Lord.

This next part may take some 'chewing' to see; to don't just reject or in a surface way accept what I'm about to show you.

Ephesians 2:4-7 (NKJV) *⁴ But God, who is rich in mercy, because of His great love with which He loved us (Jews), ⁵ even when we (Jews) were dead in trespasses, made us (Jews and Gentiles) alive together with Christ*

This next nuance, may take you a moment to even consider; let alone see. I believe, now Paul turns to the Gentiles in the room and says: *"by grace you (Gentiles) have been saved"* Paul is emphasizing their (Gentiles) inclusion in this glorious reality of being now joined to His people. This is not a correction, as it is sometimes used, but rather a kind of exhortation: *"the grace of God has done this for you, also!",* *6 and raised us* (Jews and Gentiles), *up together, and made us* (Jews and Gentiles), *sit together in the heavenly places in Christ Jesus,* *7 that in the ages to come He might show the exceeding riches of His grace in His kindness toward us (Jews and Gentiles), in Christ Jesus.* Remember to think in terms of two different groups of people Paul is addressing, and what he wants to accomplish by the Spirit of God; making them one! Don't however lose sight of this kind of 'one'; it is Jew and Gentile; distinct, but equal. It's like a man and woman being joined in marriage; distinct, but equal, coming together in a 'mystery' to become 'one' (Jew and Gentile), in a way that was never seen before. Please stop and ponder the implications of what Paul was saying as apposed to the traditional way you may have read or considered these verses. Please allow me a little latitude to allow God to put His 'golden thread' on the needle He uses to make this beautiful tapestry of life; Jew and Gentile, to be seen.

Ephesians 2:8 (NKJV) *8 For by grace you (Jew and Gentile) have been saved through faith, and that not of yourselves; it is the gift of God*

This time I believe Paul is speaking to both the Jews and Gentiles in the room (see Eph 2:6), so aware of bringing them together; what a wonderful beautiful thing it is! Paul isn't working from two thousand years of Body of

Christ history; he is functioning in his apostolic calling and God's love of the Gentiles. Paul and Holy Spirit are forming a bride of the Father's beloved Son! Again this isn't mere theology; this is 'spiritual surgery' at the highest level. A people (Gentiles) who were so 'far off' that they couldn't even have a meal with a Jew, are now being told that they are a vital and necessary part of all God had in mind from creation to all of eternity. This isn't just good information; it's the power of God accomplishing this in the hearts and minds of the Gentiles first, but also the believing Jews, whose heads must be exploding. How difficult it would be to even consider this without the presence of God in their midst! He is so good, He so understands our struggles and shortcomings, but He won't let those get in the way of the purposes of His heart. He will have a beautiful bride, without spot or wrinkle; Jew and Gentile. Even as they had to struggle with all this in practical ways, **let us not just be observers or analysts, and miss the invitation to be part of these truths today. It's all meant for us also. Don't settle for 'bullet points' when you can have encounter with God, as you take this into your heart; you have an inheritance and have been grafted into His love story, dear Gentile friend.**

Ephesians 2:9 (NKJV) *⁹ not of works, lest anyone should boast*

Now I know this is a bit of a stretch, so I'm not saying this is Paul's intent here, but I can see him turning to the Jews in the room... (you know the ones that are still capable of struggling with the Lord having these unclean Gentiles be part of this glorious expression of the Living God.) He turns his attention to them and says *"not of works, lest anyone should boast"*…you know that feeling, like you just got busted because your face is communicating what your words aren't allow to say…? Even if that's not what is going on here, just consider the amount of personal struggle it would initially take for a people, who for thousands of years were considered God's elect, and now this; the unthinkable; the impossible, is standing before them. If you are a Gentile, be sensitive as you ponder some of these scriptures to the humanity involved in all God has done and is doing even today. He is drawing forth a bride from out of the 'cloth' of the Gentile nations and His first born people; it is still a massive mystery and miracle today.

So here comes the 'chorus': ***Ephesians 2:10 (NKJV)*** [10] *For we (Jew and Gentile) are His workmanship, created in Christ Jesus for good works, which God prepared beforehand that we (Jew and Gentile) should walk in them.*

 Sing it! Shout it! But do it as a Gentile if you are a Gentile and as a Jew if a Jew; we are His workmanship; we are His workmanship! Don't miss the 'ingredient' that makes it possible; it's Jew and Gentile together! **ONE NEW MAN!**

Next comes an important "therefore"...since the above is true; you get to consider and receive what is to follow. Open wide and take this in, it's kind of like to the book of Ephesians what the 'Declaration of Independence' is to the US Constitution.

Ephesians 2:11-13 (NKJV) *[11] **Therefore** remember that you, once **Gentiles** in the flesh--who are called Uncircumcision by what is called the Circumcision (Jews) made in the flesh by hands-- [12] that at that time you (Gentiles) were without Christ, being aliens from the commonwealth of Israel (Jews) and strangers from the covenants of promise, having no hope and without God in the world. [13] But now in Christ Jesus you (Gentiles) who once were far off have been brought near by the blood of Christ.*

*Notice: it doesn't say anything about going to heaven, this life is given incredible significance and value.

I'm not even going to attempt in this short expose of mine to even begin to explore the depths of these verses. Please take time to slowly read and ponder what is being said here. Have dialogue with the Lord about what He is saying to you personally; don't worry about the theology of it. What is He saying to you about what He has accomplished in Christ Jesus for you. What has He caused to be seen upon the earth and witnessed to by the heavenly hosts? What has He accomplished to make all the realms of darkness tremble? What does this say about the value of your life and how you live it? What are you actually a part of that you have never considered before... *"the commonwealth of Israel"; "the covenants of promise": "who once were far off have been brought near by the blood of Christ"!* If this doesn't blow your mind; take your pulse. The Jewish Man Christ Jesus went to the cross to bring you Gentiles into His family! A family with history with God and all that is necessary (promises, authority, provision, life style, identity, community) to accomplish on the earth His desires for a people (Jew and Gentile), that He carries in His heart. This is what He has been waiting for you (Gentiles and Jews) to see and believe! He has accomplished this through His blood shed on the cross, for you Gentiles)! **"You (Gentiles) who once were far off have been brought near by the blood of Christ!" You (Gentiles) are no longer far off"**... It's time to ask what you have all along been meant to be a part of. Paul from the very beginning of our history as the body of Christ was telling this to the Gentiles in what he wrote. It's time to hear and receive this blessing and truth. Again, not just theology; we need to consider the practical, daily outworking of who we are (Jew and Gentile) in light of these promises. Welcome to your new "household"! **The Book of Ephesians is a love letter from God to the Gentiles**...

I hope by now if you are either a Jew or Gentile reading this, you are realizing that the Holy One of Israel has a glorious plan for both of us together; equal, but distinct.

Ephesians 2:14 (NKJV) *14 For He Himself is our peace, who has made both (Jew and Gentile) one, and has broken down the middle wall of separation*

Have you every read Ephesians and considered Paul is addressing Jews and Gentiles? Paul's mandate is not to start a new religion called 'Christianity'; he is called to convey to the Gentiles what God's heart and intention are toward them, through Jesus Christ our Messiah. Ask yourself why it matters that the dividing wall was taken down between Jew and Gentile. So what; who cares? God must! He made them (Jew and Gentile) one. Why?

Ephesians 2:15-16 (NKJV) *15 having abolished in His flesh the enmity, that is, the law of commandments contained in ordinances, so as to create in Himself one new man from the two (Jew and Gentile), thus making peace, 16 and that He might reconcile them both (Jew and Gentile) to God in one body through the cross, thereby putting to death the enmity.*

So now He has us 'together' (not across town acknowledging each other; but together); with no enmity (the state or feeling of being actively opposed or hostile to someone or something). We may not call it 'hostility', but God does… He apparently saw a need to 'fix' something we couldn't, or wouldn't. Check your heart here, or even church history; at best we have been tolerant of the Jews, or maybe felt their 'need' to get saved. Even the church's best 'face' is one of seeing the Jew as subservient, of less than. I believe the book of Ephesians is addressing that fact that we not only need each other; it 'doesn't even 'work' without each other; no it was actually never meant to be without each other! We don't need to re-write two thousand years of church history and doctrine; we need to receive the word of God into our hearts and minds.

Ephesians 2:17-18 (NKJV) *17 And He came and preached peace to you who were afar (Gentiles) off and to those (Jews) who were near. 18 For through Him we both (Jew and Gentile) have access by one Spirit to the Father.*

Here goes Paul again noting the distinction between Jew and Gentile; he wants us to see it for a reason. The next words should be able to demolish the clinical approach of theology to what He had in mind:

Ephesians 2:18 (NKJV) *18 For through Him we both (Jew and Gentile) have* **access** *by one Spirit* **to the Father**.

Why would even an earthly father want you to have access to him? What does a father ultimately want to do but love his children? So how much more does our Heavenly Father want to love us? What would change our world and us more then knowing and experiencing the love of God for each one of us personally? Jump over that 'theological wall' that wants to explain "access to the Father" and all the things you want to tell Him to do or whatever. There is a clue or 'mystery' being revealed by Paul to the ecclesia of God, through Jesus Christ our Lord; that as we stand together; one new man; Jew and Gentile, we will experience and be changed by the love of the Father towards us. We might just find this 'Christian life' might feel a bit different and our 'witness' may be more affective.

Open up wide oh Gentile friends...Ephesians 2:19-22 (NKJV)

"Now, therefore": slow down for a second and remember to ask "what is it there for?" Because of what was just said; it's like a math equation with a thousand numbers and you get to the end and see what it equals! Take a breath and take it in...

Ephesians 2:19-22 (NKJV) *¹⁹ Now, therefore you (Gentiles) are **no longer strangers** and foreigners, but*

fellow citizens *with the saints (Jews) and* **members of the household of God***,* [20] *having been built on the foundation of the apostles and prophets (Jewish leaders), Jesus Christ Himself being the chief corner stone (but all Jewish 'stones'),* [21] *in whom the whole building (Jew and Gentile), being joined together, grows into a holy temple in the Lord,* [22] *in whom you (Gentiles) also are being built together (Jew and gentile) for* **a dwelling place of God in the Spirit***.*

We aren't just here to survive and hang on until heaven or Jesus returns…we (Jew and Gentile) are being built; 'lively stones', "a dwelling place for God in the Spirit"; on the earth; in human bodies (Jew and Gentile); joined together; joined together! Have we ever seen it since the first believers? What if now is the time? Let us give Holy Spirit some access if that is what is truly upon His heart for us (Jew and Gentile), in the days the lie ahead; that He may have a holy habitation upon the earth.

So soon it may be time to take off our 'water wings' and do some swimming in the 'deeper end' of the pool…

Ephesians 3:1 (NKJV) *1 For this reason I, Paul, the prisoner of Christ Jesus for you Gentiles*

Now consider for starters what Paul in a sense is alluding to; this isn't just a ministry 'choice' that is propelling Paul forward; or religious duty. He mentions having been given the grace to work with the Gentiles of course;

love thus results, and not just power. This work is so challenging both personally and culturally, that he needs to be a "prisoner of Christ Jesus"! Even if he wanted to run and just be absorbed in the believing Jewish community, he couldn't! On one level the Father has provided His Son for the Gentiles, but He didn't stop there: He is also sacrificing a man; flesh and blood for the sake of you Gentiles. You sure must be important to the heart of God! Not to mention the difficulties that this man, Paul, must have faced within himself and from his brethren. Your value, oh Gentile brother and sister, is quite notable. Let that touch your heart, receive the love of God that was meant for you since before the foundation of the world. He must have some pretty spectacular plans for the "one new man"; Jew and Gentile, that was described in part, in chapters 1 and 2. So **Ephesians 3:1**"For this reason I, Paul"...re-read chapters 1 and 2 to begin to feel "**For this reason** I, Paul, the prisoner of Christ Jesus for you Gentiles"; you didn't just 'sneak' into the kingdom; it's the Father's heart and plan for you Gentiles to be part of this glorious reality that is going to be expressed upon the earth in the coming years.

And now a 'reminder' before Paul moves on:

Ephesians 3:3 (NKJV) [3] *how that by revelation He made known to me the **mystery** (as I have briefly written already... Ephesians 2:15-16 (NKJV) so as to create in Himself one new man from the two, thus making* peace, *¹⁶ and that He might reconcile them both to God in one body through the cross… Ephesians 2:19 (NKJV) ¹⁹ Now, **therefore**, you (Gentiles) are no longer strangers and foreigners, but **fellow citizens** with the saints (Jews) and **members of the household of God!**

Gentiles please hear this! Fellow citizens and members of the household of God; citizens live together in the same location; you are also a 'conscious' member of this special dwelling place. A 'mystery' is meant to be discovered; especially if it's been laid out for you in previous verses. And this 'mystery':

Ephesians 3:5 (NKJV) *5 which in other ages was not made known to the sons of men, as it has now been revealed by the Spirit to His holy apostles and prophets (Jews), and again: Ephesians 3:6 (NKJV) ⁶ that the **Gentiles** should be fellow heirs, of the same body, and partakers of His promise in Christ!*

 Take a breath and take it in… Now let's read the rest of the verse to find out what the 'vehicle' to communicate this truth to the world is:

Ephesians 3:6 (NKJV) *⁶ that the Gentiles should be fellow heirs, of the same body, and partakers of His promise in* Christ **through the gospel**.

Wait a minute! I thought the gospel only dealt with my sin and going to heaven! Maybe Jesus, the Father and Holy Spirit had more in mind through all Jesus did; could the reason that the blood cleanses us for all sin and unrighteousness, is 'aimed' and more than just heaven? If that's true, I need to take a 'step back' and consider what that means to me as either a Jew or a Gentile. Wow, so what <u>have</u> I been saved into? And to 'communicate' this grace given to Paul for the Gentiles:

Ephesians 3:7 (NKJV) *7 "of which I became a minister according to the gift of the grace of God given to me by the effective working of His power."*

This must take a little extra care on God's part and the 'insurance' or assurance that Paul as mere flesh and blood, will be able to work in harmony with Holy Spirit: **"the effective working of His power"**.

Bring it on!

Now let's take a look at this 'calling' of this Jewish man Paul. Some would say he got a special gift from God to accomplish what was asked of him by the Lord of Glory: he got 'delivered' from all that Jewish stuff and started a new religion called Christianity... How sad this view of Paul; and for that matter God is. How narrow and pitifully incomplete; lacking in vitality and glory of any kind. God's 'story' is so much better! Ephesians 3:8 (NKJV) *8 "To me, who am less than the least of all the saints (Jews), this grace was given, that I should preach*

among the Gentiles the unsearchable riches of Christ."
So this Jewish believer was sent especially to the
Gentiles, to bring "the unsearchable riches of Christ";
what the heck it that or those? Sounds like he is talking
about more than just going to heaven and that
whatever he has to say is 'connected' to some pretty
special things about Jesus…"unsearchable riches",
wow! But wait, there is something more connected to
Paul's responsibilities:

Ephesians 3:9 (NKJV) [9] *and to make all (Jew and
Gentile) see what is the fellowship of the mystery, which
from the beginning of the ages has been hidden in
God who created all things through Jesus Christ.*

It seems like there is a two fold, or 'connectedness'
between these two things. Could it be the "riches"
deal with identity and the "fellowship of the mystery" is
the practical outworking of what Paul is up to. We are
traditionally conditioned to think of Paul as the ultimate
theologian, and I have come to see him quite
differently. We read his words looking back on them
and try to establish universal biblical and spiritual truths,
but I feel he is speaking to people who are in bible
school trying to become theologians or preachers.
These are people who have been living in utter
darkness; separated from the covenants of God and
His people. Paul is concerned with giving them the
identity that is theirs in Christ ("the unsearchable riches

of Christ") and integrating them into the culture and expression of Jesus' believing community upon the earth ("the household of God"). When the Gentiles join this community in a real, not theoretical way; one might say it becomes "the fellowship of the mystery" that until very recently for the Gentile and Jews alike, was "hidden". You can't have fellowship in your head (of course unless you have multiple personalities or whatever), but fellowship takes others, and in this case takes both Jew and Gentiles. If you only have one or the other; you don't have fellowship of the mystery, so to speak...let that sink in.

Keep the idea of fellowship, like a tasty morsel, that you can keep in the back of your mouth and we move on in this glorious verse. Now 'get' this, **it has been hidden since the beginning of the ages!** Are you kidding me? God, through Paul's words is 'pulling back the curtain' on something that has been hidden since the beginning of time, as we measure it! (I just want to mention here, consider how many times you may have read this verse and just passed through it, without taking it in...really the implications of this verse could make us like John, when he couldn't stand in the presence of the Lord's angel.) Again, "hidden in God"; it might be worth looking at...! Just a thought here, if you made a list of things that you might think might be hidden in God since the beginning of time, probably wouldn't be the "mystery of the fellowship" (Jew and Gentile). This is just overwhelming me; "hidden in God, Who created all things through Jesus Christ", this must be so much more significant than I can even think, or try to communicate in my weak words. I am so feeling the fear of the Lord to go on, I can not do it justice, and will not even try to fully open this up. I will just 'brush up against it' a little, and I hope your spirit get stirred up, so you will pursue Holy Spirit, to take you deeper than I can.

Ephesians 3:10 (NKJV) *10 to the intent that **now** the manifold wisdom of God might be made known*

Let's move ahead in smaller pieces, "to the intent that **now**"; so you might say the purpose of the revealing of this 'mystery' is for **now.** Let's just stop for a moment and think about the implications of the "now". It's two fold, remember, Paul isn't functioning as a theologian, he is an apostle to the Gentiles; he is a shepherd to the Gentiles; he has a grace to love them and communicate the deepest things on God's heart for these new members of the 'household of God'. He is giving them value and purpose in the context of something that has never been seen or experienced before! First they have a personal encounter with the Jewish Man Christ Jesus and then they are welcomed into this foreign community that He visited as the first born of God. These Gentiles are being brought in after the Jews encountered this Jesus and became an ecclesia, and gathered together in this 'extension' of their original identity. These Gentiles that had been excluded for thousands of years; that had been considered so unclean, they couldn't even sit at the same table as the Jews and have a meal. Now they are being brought to this Jewish community as fully accepted by the God of the Jews. "Now"! it was meant to change their life style and perception of who they were. Stop and think about that, as if you were there as one of them. Also, for us looking back on what was said to them, need to consider what it means for us today. Don't let it become theology and mere truth; let it 'rock' your world, let it grab your heart; let it wreck the way you perceive what it is to be a believer. We somehow have read past these verses and haven't spent the last two thousand years growing in this reality. Just as they had a "now"; we have a "now", now! Enter in to the "now"! Now!

Ephesians 3:10 (NKJV) *[10] the manifold wisdom of God might be made known by the ecclesia;*

Did Paul, just say, *"the manifold wisdom of God"?*

Before we move on, let me do a little recap: we are dealing with a mystery that has been hidden since before time began; this mystery involves fellowship (coming together of Jew and Gentile); it has a practical outworking in the present with the authority of the God of Israel behind it; and now get this: it will cause the ecclesia to make the "manifold wisdom of God" known! Now wait a minute; this mystery involves something we in two thousand years haven't thought of, nor considered! Is that really in the bible; where has it been 'hidden'? How could God even care about what happens between Jew and Gentile, let alone wanting them together? Maybe this is important; what could it possibly look like? How inconvenient! We have been doing quite well for two thousand years without it, I think. What if we have breezed right passed and important 'ingredient' and have fallen way short of what was meant for us as His people? This is almost too much to take in; and I personally have now idea what it is supposed to look like, but I know one thing: it involves Jews and Gentiles together in fellowship! Get ready now to let the rest of the verse completely take your heart to new places. Ephesians 3:10-11 (NKJV) "He *made known by the ecclesia to the principalities and powers in the heavenly places.*" Let me try to get this: the manifold wisdom of God is to be made know to the heavenly forces all around us; not just flesh and blood; but "the principalities and powers in the heavenly places". We don't even talk or think in those terms! Are you sure He is thinking of us, maybe God had angels in mind for this task. We can hardly agree on the color of the carpet in the sanctuary... Let's also not skip over this 'little tidbit': "[11] *according to the eternal purpose which He accomplished in Christ Jesus our Lord,*". Has this ever been on your 'list' of things accomplished by Jesus? Paul said, "*according to God's eternal purpose*", that seems pretty big! Let me say it again; "*according to the eternal purpose which He accomplished in Christ Jesus our Lord,*". Is Paul, and maybe even God, 'messing' with us? How could something I have never noticed or been told about be considered "the eternal purpose of God"? We might just have to get off our camels and bed down here for a couple hundred years and just meditate on this and worship the Lord!

And if you are wondering if you can really respond:

Ephesians 3:12 (NKJV) *12 in whom we have boldness and access with confidence through faith in Him*

Exercise some of that "boldness" as you walk through the 'door' of "access" the Lord Jesus Christ has given you (Jew and Gentile); your "confidence" is not in how you feel or what you may think you know; it is in His power; the things that the Lord God Almighty has in His heart to be seen upon the earth, through earthen vessels such as ourselves; since before the foundation of the earth! Paul wants these Gentiles that God loves so much; that heaven has waited for; that the Holy One of Israel has been waiting for. These Gentile new believers, that don't know the half of what they have been brought into; these Gentiles, many of whom still have the smell of smoke upon them from their demonic sacrifices… These Gentile believers, that the unsuspecting Jewish believers are in need of to fulfill God's purposes for the whole earth. So Paul says:

Ephesians 3:13 (NKJV) *13 Therefore I ask that you do not lose heart at my tribulations for you, which is your glory.*

I believe he is not addressing the "tribulations" he had in his journeys in the book of acts; but rather the "tribulations" he suffers from his Jewish brethren; even those 'in the room' in Ephesus. Those brethren that have to get their hearts around what God is requiring of them: love for those that before were not included in "the household of God" those 'alien' Gentiles, that have always been in the grip of the realms of darkness. Those Gentiles that couldn't even be allowed at the 'table' for a meal in those Jewish homes! Paul and God are now saying to those Gentiles that have been encountered by the Lord Jesus Christ: "Come to the table; you have a place reserved for you, for all eternity!" If you are a Gentile believer, and find yourself reading this little booklet, God, the Lord of Glory, is saying to you today: **"Come to the table; you have a place reserved for you, for all eternity!" Come to the table! You have a place at the table; you are needed at the table; the Jewish believers need you!** For years we have been wringing our hands, while praying for the 'poor Jews' who rejected Jesus the Messiah, we have possibly missed the 'focus' of the Lord. He is actually addressing His Gentile friends and saying "come to the table of the Lord where your Jewish brothers are seated and waiting". Yes, many of them are in need of salvation, but there is a 'table' that has been set for two thousand years. God has whispered it to our brother Paul, who has declared it in this wonderful book, and he has had to endure the tribulations of the resistance of the 'first born of God'; the Jews, who also need to know their place at this

glorious table. Hear this, my Gentile friend, who has
been part of what you might say is the ruling class of
the church for two thousand years; this is not a Gentile
table. It is also not a table 'set' by rabbinic Judaism;
but it's the mystery of the fellowship: Jew and Gentile; a
beautiful bride! Paul saw the glory of all this for the
Gentiles, and endured much for them. In a sense,
Gentiles coming to this table is Paul's reward for his
suffering. As he said: "do not lose heart at my
tribulations for you (Gentiles), which is your glory. Yes for
your (Gentile) glory!

With this in mind, note what Paul says:

Ephesians 3:14-19 (NKJV) *14 For this reason I bow my
knees to the Father of our Lord Jesus Christ,
15 from whom the whole family (Jew and Gentile) in
heaven and earth is named, 16 that He would grant you
(Gentiles), according to the riches of His glory, to be
strengthened with might through His Spirit in the inner
man, 17 that Christ may dwell in your (Gentiles) hearts
through faith; that you (Gentiles), being rooted and
grounded in love, 18 may be able to comprehend with
all the saints (Jews) what is the width and length and
depth and height-- 19 to know the love of Christ which
passes knowledge; that you (Jew and Gentile) may be
filled with all the fullness of God.*

I don't need to comment on this; it speaks for itself. The

Father doesn't have great expectations for our behavior, but great plans for us as we enter into the mystery of this fellowship of Jew and Gentile. Rooted and grounded in love; Jew and Gentile! It produces a 'comprehension' of "what *is* the width and length and depth and height" of God and His love for us. Can you even imagine that ultimately it leads to being filled with the fullness of God! Is there any reason we shouldn't 'sign up' for this, or at least begin to ask about it? **"Come to the table!"**

In closing Paul writes this:

Ephesians 3:20-21 (NKJV) *20 Now to Him who is able to do exceedingly abundantly above all that we (Jew and Gentile) ask or think, according to the power that works in us (Jew and Gentile), 21 to Him be glory in the ecclesia by Christ Jesus to all generations, forever and ever. Amen.*

Enough said!

19 Behold, I will do a new thing, now it shall spring forth; shall you not know it? I will even make a road in the wilderness and rivers in the desert 21 This people I have formed for Myself; they shall declare My praise.

Isaiah 43:19/21 (NKJV)

NOTES

Epilogue

I quit where I did because I didn't want to get out of my 'lane'; I didn't want to go beyond the grace of God given to me in the book of Ephesians. Some of the frustration I have, is that every time I read the first 3 chapters, I feel even more that I could have said. I need to trust Holy Spirit that He is the ultimate author and if I am part of your eyes being opened to read and receive the book in a new way; He will give you the 'more' I see and beyond that, since it will be yours.

As I was reading in chapter 4 I felt I was supposed to mention some things I was feeling that couldn't be left out. So as I read those first two words of Ephesians 4: *"I therefore"*, I couldn't escape the emotions and implications of those words that Paul wrote; not as the theologian that we turned him into; but the lover that he was! A man with such a tender heart for the presence of God and the people of God that he had been given the grace to love and shepherd. So in light of all that was previously said; Paul, *"the prisoner of the Lord"* has a few words to say to those he loves. It seems to me that Paul is 'saying'; *"Don't just make note of my words; don't become experts on what was said; but live in a manner that is worthy of who you really now are in Christ; the Jewish Messiah. Do this in the humility of knowing that you who were in outer darkness and not part of the household of God, having been brought near by the very blood of Jesus, our Lord! Be gentle and patient with the Jewish believers that have to struggle with your inclusion and let love do it's work with this glorious community of Jew and Gentile. Your goal is not to take over or be lesser members, but keep the mystery of the unity of the Spirit ever before you, which will be your peace. You were brought to this place to enter into the manifold wisdom of God being expressed in this joining of Jew and Gentile. There is no other 'body' aside from the two being joined as 'one'. There is as a result of this reality (not just a truth); one hope; one Lord, Jesus Christ Himself; one faith; one baptism; one God and Father of all; Who is above all and through all, and in you (Jew and Gentile) all."*

I believe Paul is warning, especially the Gentiles here, not to go off and begin 'something new'; but in a kind of warning to be in remembrance of the spiritual reality of this body formed by Jew and Gentile. The need for a genuine fear of God, to keep these truths before them. He goes on to talk about apostles, prophets, evangelists, pastors, and teachers (all offices that existed in the Jewish community before Jesus visited them), and their function in equipping this community of believers, to grow and mature in love. The goal is more than survival or success measured in numbers, but stability in faith and ultimately reflecting the presence of the Holy One of Israel which will be manifested in love the for each other.

Ephesians 3:3-11 (NKJV) *3 how that by revelation He made known to me the mystery (as I have briefly written already, 4 by which, when you read, you may understand my knowledge in the mystery of Christ), 5 which in other ages was not made known to the sons of men, as it has now been revealed by the Spirit to His holy apostles and prophets: 6 **that the Gentiles should be fellow heirs**, of the same body, and partakers of His promise in Christ through the gospel, 7 of which I became a minister according to the gift of the grace of God given to me by the effective working of His power. 8 To me, who am less than the least of all the saints, this grace was given, that I should preach among the Gentiles the unsearchable riches of Christ, 9 and to make all see what is the fellowship of the mystery, which from the beginning of the ages has been hidden in God who created all things through*

Jesus Christ; 10 to the intent that now the manifold wisdom of God might be made known by the ecclesia to the principalities and powers in the heavenly places, 11 according to the eternal purpose which He accomplished in Christ Jesus our Lord.

Notes

<u>Notes</u>

<u>Notes</u>

Notes

Ruth's Road

www.ingramcontent.com/pod-product-compliance
Lightning Source LLC
Chambersburg PA
CBHW071422040426
42445CB00012BA/1261